# SQUIRLIE AND MAUDE

## THE WHITE SQUIRRELS OF BREVARD

### BY B. T. SCHERER

#### EDITED BY JAMES STEVICK

This book is written to provide information and motivation to readers. Its purpose is not to render any type of psychological, legal, or professional advice of any kind. The content is the sole opinion and expression of the author, and not necessarily that of the publisher.

Copyright © 2025 by B.T. Scherer.

All rights reserved. No part of this book may be reproduced, transmitted, or distributed in any form by any means, including, but not limited to, recording, photocopying, or taking screenshots of parts of the book, without prior written permission from the author or the publisher. Brief quotations for noncommercial purposes, such as book reviews, permitted by Fair Use of the U.S. Copyright Law, are allowed without written permissions, as long as such quotations do not cause damage to the book's commercial value. For permissions, write to the publisher, whose address is stated below.

Printed in the United States of America.

ISBN 978-1-64552-281-2 (Paperback)
ISBN 978-1-64552-282-9 (Hardback)
ISBN 978-1-64552-280-5 (Digital)


Lettra Press books may be ordered through booksellers or by contacting:

Lettra Press LLC
30 N Gould St. Suite 4753
Sheridan, WY 82801
1 307-200-3414 | info@lettrapress.com
www.lettrapress.com

To my father and brother
...... and all who love a Squirlie tale.

And a special thanks to my dear friend Dollie for sharing her love and knowledge of squirrels.

Hi! My name is Swish, and I'm running over to hear Grandpa's story. Come with me! He's about to begin.

Grandpa Squirrel sat on a tree stump with a baby squirrel on his lap. He asked all the little squirrels gathered at his feet, "Have you ever wondered where we came from? Would you like to hear how we came to Brevard?"

Upon hearing the squeals of delight, he cleared his throat. "All right, children. Gather round, and don't make a sound. Come sit down, here on the ground." The little squirrels giggled as Grandpa Squirrel began his story.

"It was a beautiful sunny day, many years ago. The carnival was coming to town!
Great excitement was in the air. The children knew there would be cotton candy, ice cream, and caramel apples. There would be fun games to play like the ring toss, squirt-the-duck races, and the basketball throw. Everyone wanted to win a stuffed giraffe or panda bear. And best of all, there was the parade! Everyone loved the parade, especially Sally and her brother James.

"Sally and James woke up at the crack of dawn and ate their oatmeal as fast as they could. Throwing kisses to their mother, they dashed out of the house and down to Main Street. The band was playing. The colorful trucks passed with their special cargo. The monkey car, the elephant car, the regal horses, and the ferocious tiger in his cage paraded down the street.

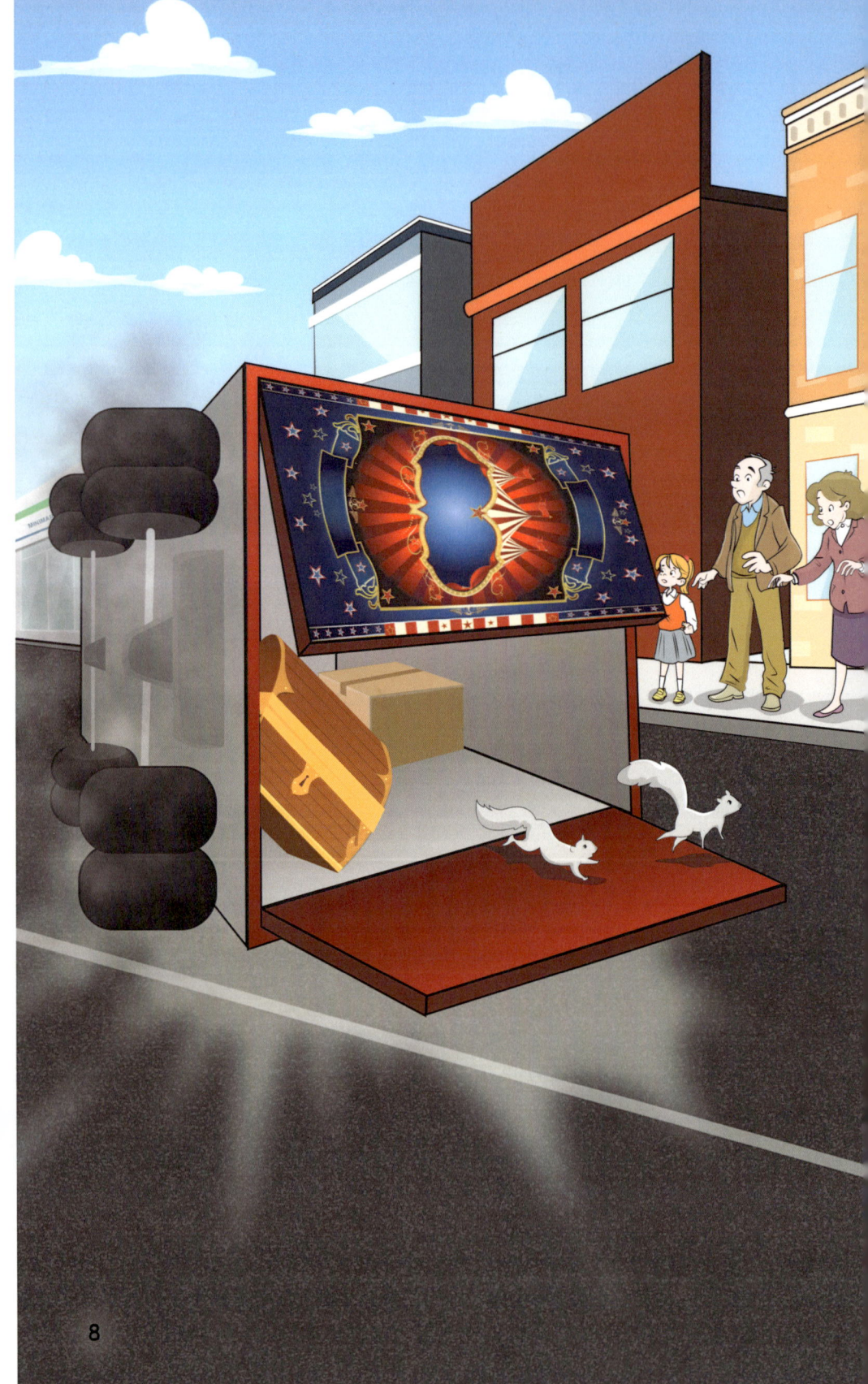

"Suddenly, a curious little girl stepped into the street to get a better look at the baby elephant peeking out from behind his mother. The man driving the carnival truck just behind the elephants was headed straight for the little girl. *Oh no! Watch out!* He slammed on the brakes as hard as he could—so hard that the truck skidded. Then it began to fall over, seemingly in slow motion, just missing the wayward child. Sally shrieked. James gasped as the truck came to rest on its side, and then muttered, 'Awesome!'

"The back door of the truck swung wide open and two little white specks ran out so quickly that only Sally and James noticed. They looked at each other and whispered, 'What was that?'"

The little squirrels around Grandpa Squirrel wanted to know, "What was it? What was it?"

Grandpa reached for an acorn, rolled it around in his paws, and winked. "It was your great-great grandparents, Squirlie and Maude! They had come all the way from Thailand to join the carnival.

"That morning, Squirlie and Maude were riding along in the carnival truck, enjoying the parade. Suddenly, they heard a loud shriek and everything went topsy-turvy. As the truck tipped over, they bumped into the ceiling and landed upside down. When the door swung open, they saw clear blue sky and leafy green trees. What did they do? They ran! They ran to the nearest tree, and up they scampered. Huffing and puffing, they hid behind a big leafy branch.

"There they sat, hearts beating fast, too scared to move a hair on their bushy white tails. Finally, they began to look around. Hanging right in front of them were hundreds of seedpods. They blinked and looked again in disbelief and delight. The trees were pecan trees, their favorite food in all the world.

"They laughed gleefully. They swished their bushy white tails and began chasing one another through the tall pecan tree. They explored every trunk, limb, and knothole, jumping from one branch to another. A strange new feeling came over them that they could do whatever they wanted. It was the wonderful feeling of freedom!

"All morning, they chased each other up and down the tree. Finally, exhausted, they stopped, hugged each other, and giggled. They could not believe their good fortune.

"Days and weeks flew by. The two happy squirrels played and ate pecans to their hearts' delight. They made friends with a wise old owl named Owlie who lived in a neighboring tree. Owlie was a fantastic story teller. They loved running over to visit him. 'Come on, Maude, let's go visit Owlie,' said Squirlie one afternoon. And off they went.

*"A-rumpity-dumpity-dumpty-dum."*

"Owlie was fast asleep and snoring. Like most owls, he was nocturnal which means he sleeps during the day and finds food at night. Awakened from his nap, he blinked and welcomed the squirrels. Being a wise owl, he loved to teach and give advice about everything and anything.

"'Do come in.' said Owlie, happy to see his new friends.

"Immediately, he launched into the meaning of the word squirrel in his deep, professorial voice. 'It so happens that the name squirrel comes from two Greek words: skia, meaning 'shadow,' and oura, meaning 'tail.' The word alludes to the squirrel sitting in the shadow of its tail.' Owlie was always using words like allude, which the young squirrels had never heard before. But they could guess the meaning from the context.

"Then Owlie warned the two little squirrels, 'Be very careful when you hide your nuts. There is a crafty bird who lives in the woods. His name is Mr. Blue Jay. He may try to steal your nuts.' Squirlie and Maude promised to be careful and off they ran to play.

"A-rumpity-dumpity-dumpty-dum."

"Sure enough, a few days later, Squirlie and Maude were out gathering nuts in their neighborhood. They began to dig a hole near an easy-to-find fallen tree. They were about to hide their nuts, when Maude swished her tail and whispered to Squirlie, 'Don't look now, but Mr. Blue Jay is watching us.'

"Using Owlie's advice, Squirlie dug a hole. But instead of dropping in the nuts, he held the nuts in his cheeks. Then he and Maude ran off to hide behind a bush to watch. They giggled as they watched Mr. Blue Jay dig up the empty hole, cock his head sideways, and look around.

"'Huh!' he grumbled to himself.

"As soon as the bird flew away, Squirlie and Maude ran over, lickity-split, to tell Owlie all about their adventure.

**"A-rumpity-dumpity-dumpty-dum.**

"Owlie answered the door and listened with wide eyes as Squirlie and Maude told him all about how they had tricked sly Mr. Blue Jay. Owlie puffed out his feathers with pride, wrapped his large wings around his little friends, and gave them a big hug.

"The days passed quickly for Squirlie and Maude. They were totally unaware that two little children had been searching every day for the little white critters they saw escape from the carnival truck. Sally and James had told no one. They heard police and carnival workers talking about the mishap, but they had remained quiet. It was their little secret! Slowly, they put together a plan to find the squirrels. They wanted to keep them as pets and they were sure their parents would allow it.

"A few weeks later, Squirlie and Maude were collecting and hiding pecans for the winter. **Wham!** Suddenly, with no warning, they were caught in a large white net.

"Oh dear," shouted the little squirrels listening to the story. "What happened next?"

Grandpa Squirrel shifted his position on the pine needles and continued. "Well, the squirrels dropped their pecans. They were not hurt but were scared.

"The children ran home with Squirlie and Maude in the net. 'Mom! Dad! Come see what we've caught!' When their parents saw the little squirrels, they exclaimed, 'Oh dear!'

"Unfortunately, Sally and James had forgotten that their father was allergic to fur. A lively family discussion ensued and after a while, a decision was made. They would take the squirrels to their Cousin Becky who lived in Brevard, North Carolina. They knew Becky loved animals, and she had time to care for the squirrels. And best of all, Sally and James could visit every summer vacation.

"The following morning, Squirlie and Maude found themselves in a large crate on the back seat of the family station wagon. During the drive from Florida to North Carolina, Sally and James sat quietly, watching the squirrels." Of course, they made time to play their favorite car games, *Going on a Picnic* and *I Spy*.

"The time flew by and soon they arrived. Cousin Becky ran out of the house with a big smile. She had been waiting for them.

"As soon as Becky saw the little squirrels, she squealed with delight. She scared the living daylights out of both Squirlie and Maude. Then she danced around the yard, doing cartwheels and jumping with joy. She had always, always wanted a pet.

"Overwhelmed with excitement and being a bit bossy, Becky immediately assigned tasks: 'James, you gather some grass and soft leaves.' and 'Sally, you find a small bowl and fill it with water.'

"The three children worked together all afternoon. They gathered soft materials including grass cuttings, crepe paper, rags, and torn-up newspaper to cover the bottom of the cage.

"Then the fun began! Carefully, they moved the tiny squirrels to their new home and sat down to watch them. Once in the new cage, Squirlie and Maude huddled close together, looking out at the children. They thought the children were adorable. They watched them scurry around all afternoon, preparing the cage, and they had to admit that they were quite happy with the results. It was soft. It was cozy. They were very comfortable except for one tiny little thing. They could not play outdoors. Squirlie's smile quickly turned upside down into a frown.

"James had an idea. 'Maybe the squirrels are hungry. I sure am.' So, the children raced to the kitchen to ask their aunt for something to feed the squirrels."

At this point, all the little squirrels listening suddenly felt hungry too. Noticing this, Grandpa Squirrel chuckled, pulled out a bunch of nuts from under his stump, and passed them out to his little listeners.

"Well," he continued while chewing on a nut. "After the children filled up on chocolate brownies and milk, they ran back to the bedroom to feed the squirrels. The children held walnuts up to the cage. Both Squirlie and Maude were very hungry and the nuts looked yummy. Timidly, they reached their tiny paws through the cage and grabbed the walnuts.

"'Yippee!' cried Becky, happy that the squirrels were eating. Then the children and the squirrels finished all the walnuts together.

"Soon it was time for Sally and James to return to Florida. They were sad saying goodbye to their cousin and the squirrels. 'Good bye! Good bye!', they cried as they drove away. They waved and waved until they were out of sight.

"What happened to Squirlie and Maude?" asked the little squirrels listening to the story.

"Well," said Grandpa Squirrel, "school began, and Becky had less and less time to spend with the squirrels. She had homework and chores to do. She started to feel sorry for the squirrels.

"And even though Squirlie and Maude were well-cared for, they were eager to return to the outdoors. They missed scavenging for nuts and playing in the trees. They missed their freedom."

"Oh dear! How sad!" piped up one little squirrel. "What did they do?"

"Squirlie and Maude decided to escape. They waited patiently for a chance. One morning, Becky's father forgot to latch the cage door and the window was open a crack, just enough for Squirlie to squeeze under. But Maude had been gaining weight and could not fit under the window. From outside on a tree branch, Squirlie swished his tail and told her not to worry.

"Every day, Squirlie visited Maude and chattered loudly. Maude peered out the window, feeling sad and lonely in the cage. She missed playing with Squirlie."

"Poor Maude," whispered the little squirrels.

Grandpa Squirrel continued, "And guess what? Happity hoppity! Two days later, Maude was set free.

"Of course, the minute Maude hopped out the window, Squirlie was there waiting for her. You can imagine the laughter and hugs of the two reunited squirrels. They chased one another up and down the tree. They were together again and free."

"Yippee! Hurray!" shouted all the little squirrels as they anticipated their favorite part of the story.

Grandpa Squirrel smiled and went on, "Finding themselves in a beautiful place with lots of nut trees, Squirlie and Maude were ready to start a family.

"It turned out that Maude was going to have babies, which is why she could not fit through the small window opening.

"Looking for a place to settle, they found a pecan grove not far from Becky's house. There were hazelnut and walnut trees, too! It was a paradise and a perfect place to make their home.

"Wasting no time, they busily made a warm, cozy nest in a tree. They scampered around happily gathering moss, leaves, grass, and feathers to soften the nest. They had learned this from the children.

"And guess what? Soon after, Maude gave birth to three itty-bitty, adorable baby squirrels: Fluffy, Muffy, and Swishy Tail."

"Awww!" whispered the little squirrels, yawning. They loved the happy ending but knew there would be a history lesson coming.

Grandpa chuckled and, sure enough, added, "We did not realize that we were unique until the day Great Grandfather Squirrel was sitting on a windowsill of the Brevard City Council Building. He overheard the commissioners talking. They were taking a vote to approve a sanctuary for all squirrels in the town.

"That day, the city council declared it wrong for people to hunt, kill, or trap any squirrel in Brevard.

"Hey!" shouted Grandpa Squirrel loudly, making all the little squirrels jump. He wanted their attention before they fell asleep. "As you may know," he continued, "some of our family settled in Tennessee and some in Kentucky, but most of us stayed right here in Brevard."

By this time, sure enough, all the little squirrels were curled up at his feet and sound asleep.

Hi again! It's me, Swish. Did you like the story? Shhhh! Let's not wake the little ones. Well, that's our history. The small town of Brevard turned out to be a safe-haven for our squirrel family. It wasn't long before our family grew into a thriving colony.

Brevard is a wonderful place. It has nut trees, beautiful waterfalls, and large farms that produce delicious crops. The people of the town are warm and friendly.

Because Brevard made us a protected species, we are delighted to give back to our town by attracting visitors. Every summer, the residents hold an annual street fair in our honor, with art, and music, and lots of family fun! And we squirrels hold a big party celebrating our great-great-grandparents, Squirlie and Maude.

So y'all hop on over to see us in Brevard!

**A-rumpity-dumpity-dumpty-dum.**

And we'll be here waiting for you. When you get here,
just look around. You will find that we
are not hard to spot!

This is
THE END

Of my TAIL and
my TALE !

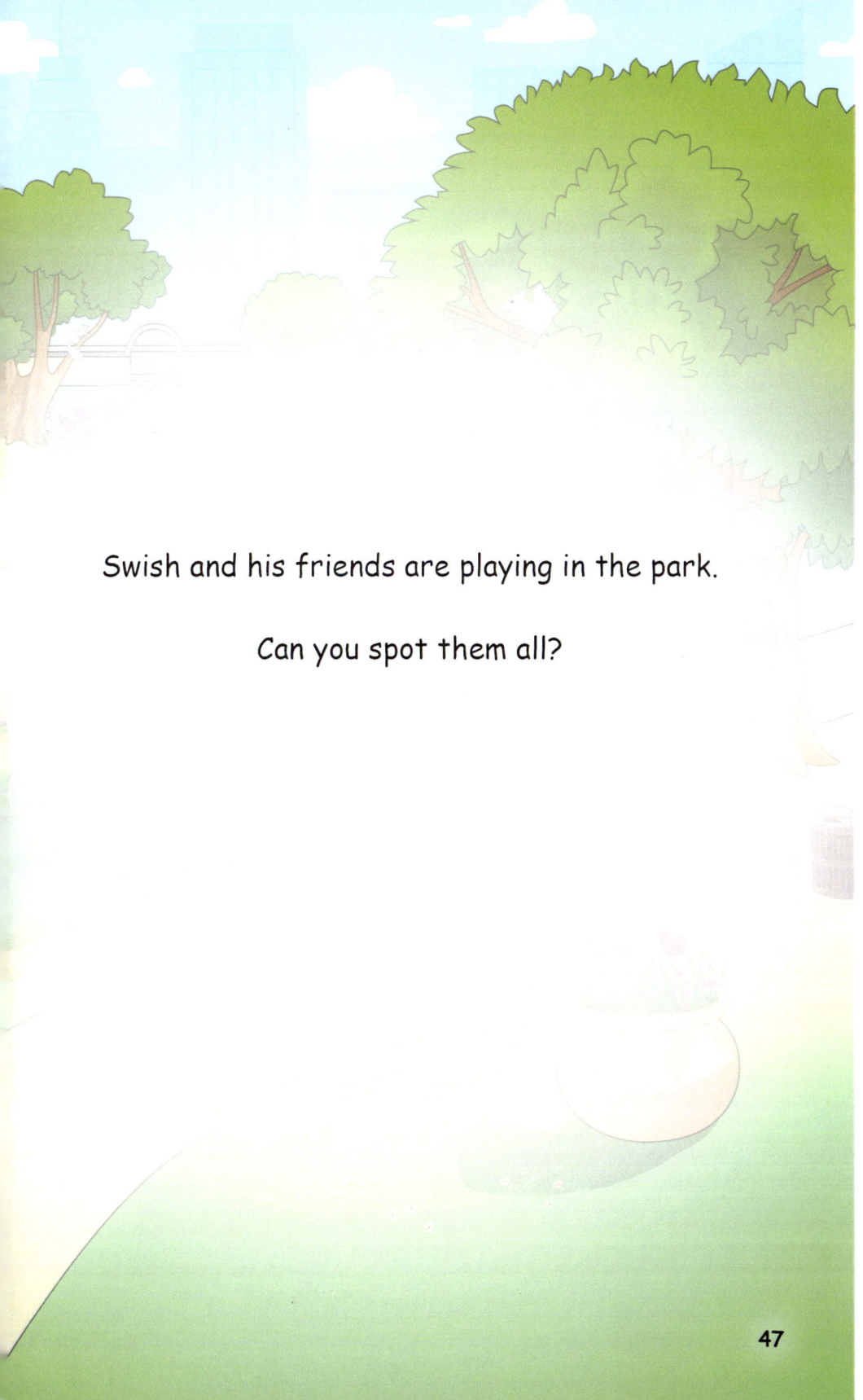

Swish and his friends are playing in the park.

Can you spot them all?

*Squirlie and Maude: The White Squirrels of Brevard*
by B.T. Scherer
Lettra Press

book review by Barbara Bamberger Scott

"A strange new feeling came over them, a feeling they could do whatever they wanted. It was the strange and wonderful feeling of freedom!"

Two rare white squirrels trapped in a carnival truck have a streak of luck when the vehicle overturns, and the door falls open. This is the beginning of the tale woven by Grandpa Squirrel to his grandchildren, who listen with rapt attention as he describes how Squirlie and Maude, their ancestors from Thailand, arrive in Florida and are adopted by two children who give them a decent home, keeping them as pets in a small cage. Gradually, though, it seems their cousin in Brevard, North Carolina, can provide a better habitat for the pair. Content but still encaged, the little white wonders manage an escape into the trees and parks. They have many adventures and, soon, three babies Fluffy, Muffy, and Swishy Tail. Eventually, the city council makes Brevard a sanctuary for the adorable white creatures. As Grandpa Squirrel concludes his story, his white squirrel listeners are curled up at his feet and sound asleep.

Author Scherer, a student of biology and ecology, has created this marvelous tale inspired by stories told to her in her childhood. She has deftly combined fiction and fact. There are rare white squirrels famously inhabiting Brevard. They did originally come from a carnival in Florida and may have originated in Thailand. Of course, their enjoyable antics with a food-stealing blue jay and a wise old owl are touches from the writer's lively imagination. Scherer demonstrates her clear wish to entertain and gently inform her young audience. Meanwhile, illustrations by Lettra Press brings the squirrel saga to life with large, colorful action scenes on nearly every page. Scherer's book has the power to delight young readers with its furry, friendly characters and to engage those who read with and to them. Its easily accessible, factual background adds an extra layer of interest.

www.ingramcontent.com/pod-product-compliance
Lightning Source LLC
LaVergne TN
LVRC091352060526
838200LV00034B/495